THE LITTLE BLACK BOOK OF
MOTORCYCLE WISDOM

THE LITTLE BLACK BOOK OF
MOTORCYCLE WISDOM

Edited by

MALCOLM NELSON

FOREWORD BY KRISTEN LASSEN

Skyhorse Publishing

Skyhorse Publishing books may be purchased in bulk at special discounts for sales promotion, corporate gifts, fund-raising, or educational purposes. Special editions can also be created to specifications. For details, contact the Special Sales Department, Skyhorse Publishing, 307 West 36th Street, 11th Floor, New York, NY 10018 or info@skyhorsepublishing.com.

Skyhorse® and Skyhorse Publishing, Inc.®, are registered trademarks of Skyhorse Publishing, Inc.®, a Delaware corporation.

Visit our website at www.skyhorsepublishing.com.

10 9 8 7 6 5 4 3 2

Library of Congress Cataloging-in-Publication Data is available on file.

ISBN: 978-1-5107-4058-7
Ebook ISBN: 978-1-5107-4060-0

Cover design by Tom Lau

Printed in China

CONTENTS

FOREWORD

I came back to reality with sunburns etched into odd patches of my body. A band of bright red wrapped around my wrists and ankles. It was a surefire topic of the day. I had just ridden over a thousand miles in eighteen hours on my motorcycle in order to make it back for the start of my senior year in high school. Refocusing into routine was quite the buzzkill after traveling five thousand exhilarating miles to South Dakota.

Known as the "mecca" of motorcycling, the Sturgis Motorcycle Rally in South Dakota unfolded a culture and landscape that my raw mind had never before experienced. My body would send goosebumps over my skin, mimicking the miles of topography shifts that lay before me. There was a vast assortment of riders and motorcycles making the journey north to the event itself. Every pocket of the culture created a mosaic of personalities carrying frequencies much different from those of their neighbors. You would find a leather-clad one-percenter in the same stroke as a leather-clad flat track racer. No matter the history of your motorcycle journey, you were accepted there. You were a vital part of the thriving culture.

Riding a motorcycle is truly transformative. It is an external high that caresses your being, melting away the weight that may lie on your back. I came to believe it when motorcycling began to creep into every facet of my being when I reached the ripe age of seventeen. The machines became the metaphorical (and quite literal) vehicle that led me down every road since throwing my leg over.

I am Kristen Lassen. I am a fourth-generation rider. I've carried on the adrenaline of my great-grandfather's Wall of Death stints. I've carried on the wanderlust of my grandfather, who joined the Navy and cruised all over the Earth's beautiful lands. I've carried on my father's curiosity about the build and nature of the machine itself. In turn, I resonate with the lawless speed demon, the itching explorer, and the meticulous mechanic. It has stretched me into a community with as many backgrounds as there are stars in the sky.

Ever since, every decision has circled right back to my motorcycle. I've taken a cross-country trip every year, competed in races, and worked as a motorcycle mechanic. I've developed as a human through the interactions with the man, the machine, and all that it encompasses.

Foreword

The Little Black Book of Motorcycle Wisdom aptly reflects these kinds of strings of interactions. More than quotes, they are musings built on the range of emotions that motorcycles can provide people. From the collage of motorcycles and their riders, a new journey awakens in each tale. Roll forward and enjoy the ride.

Kristen Lassen

PART ONE

THE URGE TO RIDE

The world's magnificence has been enriched by a new beauty: the beauty of speed.
—FILIPPO TOMMASO MARINETTI (1909)

• • •

Hurrah for the poetry of machines, propelled and driving; the poetry of levers, wheels, and wings of steel.
—DZIGA VERTOV (1922)

• • •

Being shot out of a cannon will always be better than being squeezed out of a tube. That is why God made fast motorcycles. . . .
—HUNTER S. THOMPSON

• • •

God didn't create metal so that man could make paper clips!
—HARLEY-DAVIDSON AD

• • •

Four wheels move the body. Two wheels move the soul.
—ANONYMOUS

• • •

I love it because when you ride a [motor]bike, there's so much danger about it that all your instincts come right to the surface, all your senses.
—JEREMY IRONS

• • •

As I ride away to the west, the noise in the engine seems to settle in a rhythmic thrum, and the wind ripples the grass in the fields alongside the road. The tops of the blades are waving to and fro, and it's easy to imagine the valves in the engine rising and falling with them, in sync with nature.
—MARK RICHARDSON

• • •

The key is turned; the green and red idiot lights glow. The starter button on the right handlebar, pressed, begins a whirling below. A simultaneous twist of the right grip pulls the throttle cables, and the engine gulps, then roars. . . . The rider pulls in the left-hand lever, then presses down with the left toe. There's a solid chunk as first gear engages. The bike moves forward, into a brighter world.
—MELISSA HOLBROOK PIERSON

• • •

Sometimes it takes a whole tankful of fuel before you can think straight.
—Motorcycle T-shirt

• • •

After I saw *The Wild One*, I knew I wanted a real motorcycle.
—Sonny Barger

• • •

We wanna be free! We wanna be free to do what we wanna do. We wanna be free to ride our machines without being hassled by The Man. . . . And we wanna get loaded.
—Peter Fonda as Captain America in *Easy Rider*

• • •

One of the things that makes motorcycling so great is that it never fails to give you a feeling of freedom and adventure.
—STEVE MCQUEEN

• • •

I think the motorcycle is best because it puts us so much in contact with everything. You experience much more closely the nature of the terrain. Almost taste the cultures that you are riding through. Because it exposes you to the climate and to wind and rain, it's a much more complete experience.
—TED SIMON

• • •

I take good care of myself. I eat a healthy diet, I exercise every day, and I ride safe. I do this not because I'm afraid of dying. I do it because the longer I stay healthy, the longer I can ride motor-cycles.
—SONNY BARGER

• • •

I'm in a position where I can do many things most people just daydream about. But I find doing something like this [a long motorcycle trip] puts my whole life into relief. You understand yourself better and are more available to the world.
—EWAN MCGREGOR

• • •

Every time I start thinking the world is all bad, then I see people having a good time riding motorcycles and it makes me take another look.
—STEVE MCQUEEN

• • •

Hey sweetheart! You want to see how a movie is made?
—STEVE MCQUEEN TO TWENTY-YEAR-OLD LAUREN HUTTON AS HE RODE BY ON AN INDIAN MOTORCYCLE

• • •

A motorcycle functions entirely in accordance with the laws of reason, and a study of the art of motorcycle maintenance is really a miniature study of the art of rationality itself.
—Robert M. Pirsig

• • •

An excellent match, freedom and power. Horses and horsepower. Riding a horse at a full gallop is exhilarating, but a motorcycle lets you go where you want. You're not closed in a box, everything around you is alive, the trees, the mountains, the sea. You're in tune, you're one with your surroundings and your machine, enjoying all five senses like you've never experienced in your life.
—Michael Fassbender

• • •

I ride horses, and the motorbike gives you similar freedom.
You're very in touch with all your senses, and it's quite dangerous.
So you have to concentrate.
—JEREMY IRONS

• • •

[I]t's turned into just about a perfect day to be going someplace
on a motorcycle. . . . A car goes by carrying a driver in a white
shirt and tie. He could be a salesman on the way to a call, or an
office worker returning from lunch. As he passes, he stares in
our direction. I can practically see him mouth the words: "Lucky
jerks."
—BILL WOOD

• • •

When I leave work on a motorbike, pull on my helmet and move off, it doesn't matter if I've had a good day or not.
—Ewan McGregor

• • •

The function of this club is to have fun, to have brotherly love, and to ride on our motorcycles and be free.
—"Love," president of the Black Falcons Motorcycle Club (1978)

• • •

Riding a motorcycle is essentially a solitary pursuit. . . . Yet motorcycling can also be a most sociable hobby. Wherever in the world there are bikes, there are riders who congregate to compare machines, modifications, and cornering lines; to swap information, spare parts, and tall stories.

—ROLAND BROWN

• • •

[W]e are individualists, but also a sociable lot. You can be big, small, black, white, gay, straight, Martian, blue-eyed, green-eyed, long-haired, short-haired, abled, disabled, cat loving, dog loving, or what not. If you're on a motorcycle, you're welcome anywhere.

—BARBARA ANN MAHONEY, LETTER TO THE EDITOR,
THE NEW YORK TIMES

• • •

I was rocketing through the New Mexico desert's pre-dawn light. My only source of company and comfort in this dark and desolate landscape was the machine I was astride. The big Suzuki was howling at wide-open throttle, singing in ecstasy at doing what it was created for.
—DANIEL MEYER,
FROM *LIFE IS A ROAD, THE SOUL IS A MOTORCYCLE*

• • •

You can forget what you do for a living when your knees are in the breeze.
—ANONYMOUS

• • •

On to the freeway now, dodging the traffic on the inside lane over the brow of the Anzac Bridge and down the other side, blue water twinkling below, white boats bobbing about on the surface. I loved this part of the journey, flat out . . . weaving between cars and lorries.
—NATHAN MILIWARD, FROM *THE LONG RIDE HOME*

• • •

I'm pretty sure this was the day I decided to jack it all in and head off on my motorcycle. . . . Most of all I wanted to be moving along, to always be going somewhere. It's as old as mankind, the urge to roam, but when you get it and succumb to it, for a fleeting moment you kind of feel like you invented it.
—LOIS PRYCE, FROM *LOIS ON THE LOOSE*

• • •

One of the reasons I have always loved motorcycling is that it gives me time to think—time without the distractions of the telephone or other day-to-day interruptions. AMA Board Member Dal Smilie notes that when he rides he is able to think so clearly that he develops solutions for all of the world's major problems. Unfortunately, he notes, those solutions always vanish when he turns off the key and parks his bike.
— JOHN VAN BARRIGER

• • •

Driving a motorcycle is like flying. All your senses are alive. When I ride through Beverly Hills in the early morning, and all the sprinklers have turned off, the scents that wash over me are just heavenly.
—HUGH LAURIE

• • •

Most of it was just good, clean fun, like drinking beer all night and standing up on the seat of your motorcycle, drunk and without a helmet, at three o'clock in the morning, while you blew every light on Hempstead Turnpike.
—JOHN HALL, FROM *RIDING ON THE EDGE*

• • •

Only a motorcyclist knows why dogs stick their heads out of car windows.
—ANONYMOUS

• • •

Riding a motorcycle is technology's closest equivalent to being a cowboy. Our modern horse has two wheels instead of four. . . . Its reins are the handlebars, its stirrups the clutch and brake—its rider (hopefully) sufficiently experienced with the laws of nature to skillfully control his excitable steed.
—ROBERT EDISON FULTON JR.

• • •

On my tombstone they will carve, "IT NEVER GOT FAST ENOUGH FOR ME."
—HUNTER S. THOMPSON

• • •

To those who love motorcycles deeply, there is usually one aspect of the machine that broadcasts its allure in advance of all others. . . . For me, it is their sound that makes the heart race.
—MELISSA HOLBROOK PIERSON

• • •

[While riding in a car] you're a passive observer and it is all moving by you boringly in a frame. . . . [O]n a cycle the frame is gone. You're completely in contact with it all. You're in the scene, not just watching it anymore, and the sense of presence is overwhelming.
—ROBERT M. PIRSIG

• • •

Part of the joy of motorcycling is that you are not enclosed in a "cage," as in a car. In fact, hard-core biker types often refer to cars as "cages" for this reason.
—DAVE PRESTON, FROM *MOTORCYCLE 201*

• • •

One of the great advantages of the motorcycle is its ability to bring its rider close to the environment—winds, weather, roads, surroundings, nature.
—ROBERT EDISON FULTON JR.

• • •

If the wind does you good, you're welcome with us.
—HARLEY RIDER

• • •

Motorcycles bring people together. Motorcycles are like being naked. Just as everyone exists on the same level naked, riding one unites you with other riders, whether they be mechanics or stock brokers, professors or construction workers. . . . The sensation of being on a motorcycle embodies what we're all seeking in life. Freedom.
—FROM THE *International Journal of Motorcycle Studies*

• • •

Motorcycle riders are motion addicts. And only other riders truly understand the affliction.
—James Hesketh, from *Riding a Straight and Twisty Road*

• • •

I enjoy the sensual intimacy with nature when I'm on the bike. I'm in tune with my surroundings, the temperatures, the smells.
— JAY HOLECEK, A KAWASAKI KLR 650 RIDER

• • •

There's something about going riding with your friends—a feeling of freedom, a feeling of joy—that really can't be put into words. It can only be fully shared by someone who's done it.
—BRUCE BROWN, FROM *ON ANY SUNDAY*

• • •

Riding fast on a motorcycle is a tremendously exhilarating and challenging game. . . . There's something to win, something to lose, and a purpose for each individual who plays the game. It demands your attention. The consequences of a major mistake can be severe—severe enough to make the game worth playing well.
—KEITH CODE

• • •

Motorcycling is a deeply embodied experience and its pleasures, like those of sex, are exceedingly difficult to communicate, whether through prose or visually.
—STEVEN ALFORD AND SUZANNE FERRISS, FROM *MOTORCYCLE*

• • •

Kicking it with your peeps, wearing tacky threads you would never really wear ever at home (ever), driving a fully loaded Harley and knocking back some ice cold Bud in the middle of God D**n America, is really what life is all about at the end of the day, isn't it?
—STACIE KRAJCHIR-TOM

• • •

A motorcycle is whatever you want to make it. Turn it on and you'll give yourself a real thrill.
—BRUCE BROWN

• • •

In the all-you-can-eat Chinese buffet that is motorcycling, there are dishes to please everybody; find the one that you like . . . and you will return to fill your plate again and again. Off-road; adventure touring; Sunday cruising; canyon racing. All of these are understood, if not preeminently loved, by most riders.
—MELISSA HOLBROOK PIERSON

• • •

It was very calm.
—BILL WARNER, AFTER SETTING THE MOTORCYCLE WORLD LAND SPEED RECORD IN 2011, REACHING A SPEED OF 311.945 MILES PER HOUR IN 1.5 MILES, DESCRIBING THE SENSATION AT TOP SPEED

• • •

It was a little scary.
—BILL WARNER, DESCRIBING WHAT IT WAS LIKE TRYING TO
STOP HIS MOTORCYCLE AFTER REACHING TOP SPEED

• • •

One of the great things about riding a motorcycle is that it's a
constant exercise in skill management.
—ALTON BROWN

• • •

[Motorcycle] racing is life. Anything that happens before or after
is just waiting.
—STEVE MCQUEEN

• • •

When my mood gets too hot and I find myself wandering beyond control, I pull out my motor-bike and hurl it top-speed through these unfit roads for hour after hour. My nerves are jaded and gone near dead, so that nothing less than hours of voluntary danger will prick them into life. . . .
—T. E. Lawrence

• • •

That's all the motorcycle is, a system of concepts worked out in steel.
—Robert M. Pirsig

• • •

To ride well, you have to have control over your mind at all times
and to be able to feel your control over the bike.
—MALCOLM SMITH

• • •

Riding, to me, at really fast speeds is my own high. . . . You're
right at the top of things, when you're right at the edge of
crashing. There's no feeling like it.
—MALCOLM SMITH

• • •

Ride it like you stole it!
—MOTORCYCLE T-SHIRT

• • •

[A] motorcycle can change the conduct and quality of our lives because it is indeed a machine that can harness a man's spirit. On a motorcycle, riding the road, hugging the wind, a man can discover the joy of solitude, the rebirth of independence, the satisfaction of self-respect.
—LEE GUTKIND, FROM *BIKE FEVER*

• • •

Here we are, two childless (not by choice) forty-somethings with no ties and the desire to leave Australia after twelve years. What better way to do this than to ride our motorbikes?
—KATE MACDONELL,
FROM *FROM WOLLONGONG TO WOOLWICH*

• • •

I graduated with a degree in theology and wanted to go to my spiritual home [Rome]. That all changed in the briskly cool month of November 2002. I sat in a monastery refectory . . . when a sudden, rushing urge came upon me to take a motorcycle ride. Not a little ride around the state of North Dakota, but a ride around the states. . . . My spiritual journey would take place, to be sure, but in a very different manner.
—BRYAN PECHTL, FROM *OF MOTORCYCLES AND BROTHERS*

• • •

With loneliness comes a certain freedom. Freedom enables mobility and independence. There. I had a new tripod. And what embodies these three elements better than a motorcycle?
—Jeremy Kroeker, from *Motorcycle Therapy*

• • •

I rode for the enjoyment of safely completing the most difficult motorcycle rally on the planet, and to enjoy the camaraderie of this group of exceedingly atypical folk who love riding endless miles for no other reason than the ride itself.
—Joel Rappoport, from *Hopeless Class*

PART TWO

• • •

BIKES AND THE RIDERS WHO LOVE THEM

For much of society, the motorcycle remains a forbidden indulgence, an object of fascination, fantasy, and danger. Park the latest Ducati, Harley, Honda, or BMW on a street corner in any city or town in the world and a crowd will gather.
—FROM THE CATALOG FOR "THE ART OF THE MOTORCYCLE" EXHIBIT AT THE GUGGENHEIM MUSEUM IN NEW YORK CITY

• • •

This is my first visit here. I don't go to museums a lot, and it will probably be a long while before I ever come back.
—A YOUNG MOTORCYCLE MECHANIC AS HE ENTERED "THE ART OF THE MOTORCYCLE" EXHIBIT AT THE GUGGENHEIM MUSEUM

• • •

My experience with motorcycles has only been the loud noise they make on the street. But I'm learning. They're really very beautiful machines.
—AN EIGHTY-ONE-YEAR-OLD WOMAN AT THE GUGGENHEIM EXHIBIT

• • •

Motorcycles are such a document of our time. When you think of the early years of this century, you think of the beginning of the machine age.
—DENNIS HOPPER

• • •

I can think of no nobler a calling than to protect, promote, and preserve the heritage of motorcycling for generations to come.
—JEFFREY V. HEININGER, CHAIRMAN, AMERICAN MOTORCYCLE HERITAGE FOUNDATION

• • •

For most of the world, a motorcycle is a practical, inexpensive means of transport. To understand the motorcycle as a consequence of purpose-driven design, we need to think globally while riding locally.
—STEVEN ALFORD AND SUZANNE FERRISS, FROM *MOTORCYCLE*

• • •

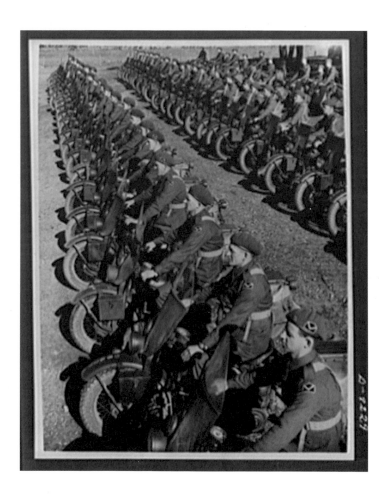

Before the automobile, there was the motorcycle. And even after, with most pre-Ford auto manufacturers focusing on an elite class of customers, it was the motorcycle that put the world on wheels.
—ED YOUNGBLOOD

● ● ●

Records show that as many as forty thousand motorcycles were sent by America to the Russian Army to help them battle the Germans during World War II.
—TOM COTTER

● ● ●

Motorcycle riding gets you out in the fresh air. Smell real pine trees, not the scent of a pine-shaped deodorizer hanging from the mirror.
—PAUL CROWE

• • •

Ahh, it is an excellent motorcycle but it is not very good.
—MICHAEL GLENNON IN *MOTORCYCLE KARMA*

• • •

The bikes had a hypnotic effect on me. I loved to look at them; there was something in their design that seemed perfect. In fact, during that period nothing seemed so nearly perfect as those steel and chrome motorcycles. . . . The fact that they actually ran was a secondary feature. I would have been satisfied to have one in my living room as an *objet d'art*.
—RICHARD LA PLANTE, FROM *HOG FEVER*

• • •

You're the guy that'll be sneaking out of your bedroom at three o'clock in the morning to look at your bike.
—PAUL TEUTEL SR., OF *AMERICAN CHOPPER*

• • •

You can fit three or four bikes into the space occupied by one car.
Make maximum use of a small garage, buy motorcycles.
—Paul Crowe

• • •

There are handlebars and a seat, true. Yet, at its essence, a motor-cycle is an engine between two wheels.
—Kris Palmer

• • •

I had to paint it. It wouldn't attract any girls.
—The owner of a Harley-Davidson that had originally been purchased by the US military and painted olive drab

• • •

You can imagine someone in a tweed suit and cap riding it through the Cotswolds.
—EWAN MCGREGOR, ON HIS 1956 SUNBEAM S7 DELUXE

• • •

Being unrestored was the main appeal.
—THE OWNER OF A 1925 ROYAL ENFIELD

• • •

They say you never want a bike built on Friday. I think this engine was built about ten minutes before closing on a Friday afternoon.
—THE NEW OWNER OF A FORTY-YEAR-OLD 650 BSA

• • •

In a sweep of the eye you can see that these 1940 Harley-Davidsons are new! They are distinct, different, streamlined, and breathe the spirit of speed and power.
—A COMPANY BULLETIN, 1940

• • •

George . . . would like to know how much this [Ducati 748] is costing you. George . . . would like to buy it for you.
—GEORGE LUCAS'S RIGHT-HAND MAN TO EWAN MCGREGOR DURING THE FILMING OF *STAR WARS EPISODE ONE*

• • •

[In the early twentieth century], automobile prices were beyond the reach of most middle-class Americans, and the $200 Harley-Davidson was touted as reliable transportation.
—TOD RAFFERTY, FROM *HARLEY-DAVIDSON: THE ULTIMATE MACHINE*

• • •

Magnificently sleek styling, flashing chrome, and
striking two-tone color combinations command
immediate attention wherever you go.
—HARLEY-DAVIDSON AD (1957)

• • •

The Hell's Angels seem to have a preference for large heavy-duty
American-made motorcycles.
—FROM THE CALIFORNIA ATTORNEY GENERAL'S REPORT,
"THE HELL'S ANGELS MOTORCYCLE CLUB"

• • •

We have a code of ethics, despite what society may think.
Besides, in the movie they showed us riding Hondas. Everybody
knows that the Hell's Angels don't ride anything but
Harley-Davidsons.
—George Christie, president of the Ventura, California,
chapter of the Hell's Angels, commenting on a
trademark lawsuit against filmmaker Roger Corman

• • •

Harley-Davidson wouldn't comp us bikes for *Easy Rider* because
the protagonists were outlaws and they thought it was bad for
their image.
—Dennis Hopper

• • •

One year, [my brother] Gregg got a guitar for Christmas and I got me a Harley 165 motorcycle. I tore that up and he learned to play. He taught me and I traded the wrecked bike parts for another guitar.

—DUANE ALLMAN

• • •

A person can purchase a Harley-Davidson and then participate in this grand tradition of playing the cowboy rather than riding on his steed; he can ride on his iron horse out into the open Interstates of the United States.

—STEVEN ALFORD

• • •

The [Harley-Davidson] brand itself has generated such intense loyalty, even aggressive loyalty. I can't really think of another brand which is maybe so often tattooed on the bodies of its owners and enthusiasts.
—JAY ALLISON

• • •

To many people in America, a motorcycle *is* a Harley-Davidson.
—SUZANNE FERRISS

• • •

Hey, you know what, that's my bike. . . . I took my own sweat and imagination and put everything I had into it. That guy who's got enough sense to have a license ought to watch out. If he hits my bike, that's on him. If we don't get him in front of the house, we'll get him on the corner.
— SANDY ALEXANDER, HELL'S ANGELS CHAPTER PRESIDENT (1971)

• • •

I don't know about the Honda or the Kawasaki guys, but we don't leave a man behind. Ever. And that's what Harley's all about.
—A HARLEY RIDER

• • •

I think if Jesus came back today, he'd probably ride [a Harley].
—DEACON DAVE AKIN

• • •

$20,000 and 2000 Miles Does Not Make You a Biker.
—STICKER ADORNING THE HELMET OF A HARLEY RIDER

• • •

I rode British motorcycles all through the Sixties, when they were the hot item—and regular maintenance meant getting out the tool kit (large) and going over all the many nuts, bolts, and screws once a week, every day if I was traveling.
—CLEMENT SALVADORI

• • •

Yers truly . . . has hardly ever been without some form of late-1960s Triumph in the garage. I like the way these bikes look and sound, but there's more to it than that. Part of their appeal lies in the fact that these are the bikes I most lusted after during the time I was in Vietnam. And every time I look at one now, it reminds me I'm back. There's a little reward built into every Triumph, a little private celebration.
—PETER EGAN

• • •

A wise man once said that the only way to prevent a British motorcycle from leaking is not to put oil in it.
—TOM COTTER

• • •

I hadn't been on a [Triumph] Bonneville for a couple of years and had forgotten what a delightful, all-purpose standard motorcycle it is.
—PETER EGAN

• • •

There is surely some powerful lesson in the failure of Harley-Davidson to keep pace with a market they once controlled entirely. . . . A monopoly with a strong protective tariff should be in a commanding position even on the yo-yo market. How would the yo-yo maker feel if he were stripped, in less than a decade, of all his customers except Hell's Angels and cops?
—*SATURDAY EVENING POST* (1965)

• • •

You meet the nicest people on a Honda.
—HONDA AD (1963)

• • •

What Honda did by producing the CB750 [in 1969] was the
equivalent of a car company producing a high-quality sports car
equal to or better than . . . Porsche or Mercedes, and then selling
it for the price of a Hyundai.
—DARWIN HOLMSTROM

• • •

If you want to be happy for a year, marry. If you want to be happy
for a lifetime, ride a BMW.
—BMW AD (1965)

• • •

Used motorcycles fall into two categories: bargains and nightmares.
—LEE GUTKIND

• • •

The Ducati 900 is a finely engineered machine. . . . The nasty little bugger looked like it was going 90 miles an hour when it was standing still in my garage.
—HUNTER S. THOMPSON

• • •

Did I mention that [Ducatis] are slightly impractical and mildly uncomfortable? So why do we keep coming back to them? . . . We don't need them. But then we don't need red wine, pungent cigar smoke, or Italian opera, either.
—PETER EGAN

• • •

The ultimate bike for the smaller rider, in any of its iterations, is the Ducati Monster, a perfect example of a naked standard moto. Narrow bars, lower seat height, feather weight, wasp-waist, quick responsive engine and handling. . . .
—ANN DALY, FROM "FOR THE LADIES: A BIKE FOR THE SHORT CHICK"

• • •

I'd always favored the lighter KTM over the BMW.
—CHARLEY BOORMAN

• • •

KTM is the Rolling Stones. Everything else is Take That.
—CHARLEY BOORMAN

• • •

The BMW is practical, because they absolutely f***ing do what
they're meant to do. Which is keep going.
—Ewan McGregor

• • •

Today's machines are filled with wizardry so that they're more
powerful, more responsive, and more reliable—so that they get
you wherever it is you're going even faster. They still break down,
but their high-tech parts often can't be fixed without a software
patch: all you can do is hope a nearby shop will be able to replace
the piece.
—Mark Richardson

• • •

[The new] Indian Chieftain . . . [is] a bike made for longer comfortable rides with a power windshield, hard saddlebags featuring
remote locks, and a high-output audio system featuring inte-
grated Bluetooth smartphone connectivity.
— JEFF ENGEL, *THE BUSINESS JOURNAL SERVING GREATER
MILWAUKEE*

• • •

What do a golden retriever and a [insert name of least favorite
motorcycle brand] have in common?

They both spend lots of time in the backs of pickup trucks.
—OLD JOKE

• • •

There's no better reason for a fifty-two-year-old woman to get a motorcycle other than to accessorize her cherry red lipstick.
—DIANA BLETTER, FROM *THE MOM WHO TOOK OFF ON HER MOTORCYCLE*

• • •

If she changes her oil more than she changes her mind, follow her.
—BUMPER STICKER

• • •

The Enfield, I've realized, is really a temperamental women disguised as a motorcycle and ours is not a relationship of convenience.
—AJIT HARISINGHANI, FROM *ONE LIFE TO RIDE*

• • •

The baby boomers are getting older, man. People riding all their lives don't want to stop just because of bad knees, or bad eyes, or diabetes or something. They want to keep rocking.
—"FAT DADDY" STIREWALT, ON THE GROWING POPULARITY OF THREE-WHEELED MOTORCYCLES

• • •

We emerged into a square lined with Renaissance-era buildings and saw four late-model BMW motorcycles parked in a tidy row in front of a single open restaurant. . . . Two of the bikes were 1100s, made in 1999. I felt my first twinge of motorcycle envy.
—ELISABETH EAVES

• • •

Sure, I dream . . . for a stroker. About fourteen hundred CCs worth. Tucked into a '74 straight-legged chromed frame kicked—with sixteen-inch mag rear wheel—with a chromed sprocket; a chromed chain; chromed spokes; a chrome tranny; a chrome footy; and a eight-inch extended Sportster fork with a chromed dog-bone.
—BILLY GREEN BUSH AS ZIPPER IN *ELECTRA GLIDE IN BLUE*

• • •

Why not ride an Indian? You will envy the fellow who has one.
—INDIAN AD (1914)

• • •

For many years . . . you could buy a new [Harley-Davidson] bike
and turn around and sell it that same day for a profit. But those
days are long gone.
—SONNY BARGER

• • •

You can plan on building a Harley four or five times before a
Honda wears out.
—SONNY BARGER

• • •

My bike has all the amenities but the kitchen sink.
—A HONDA GOLD WING RIDER

• • •

From my mother I learned to write prompt thank-you notes . . . ;
from Mrs. King's ballroom dancing school I learned a proper
curtsy and, believe it or not, what to do if presented with nine
eating utensils at the same place setting, presumably at the home
of the host to whom I had just curtsied. From motorcycles I
learned practically everything else.
—MELISSA HOLBROOK PIERSON

• • •

A skittish motorbike with a touch of blood in it is better than all
the riding animals on earth, because of its logical extension of
our faculties, and the hint, the provocation, to excess conferred
by its honeyed untiring smoothness.
—T. E. LAWRENCE

• • •

Close up the motorcycle looked even better than he expected. It was new and shiny and had a good set of tires. Ralph walked all around it, examining the pair of chromium mufflers, the engine and the hand clutch. . . . Feeling that this was an important moment in his life, he took hold of the handgrips.
—FROM *THE MOUSE AND THE MOTORCYCLE*, BY BEVERLY CLEARY

• • •

There was so much power the front wheel was getting airborne out of the turns.
—THE NEW OWNER OF A 1941 INDIAN SCOUT RACER AFTER HE TOOK THE BIKE ON ITS FIRST RIDE IN MORE THAN FIFTY YEARS

• • •

When we met, it was like we had known each other for years. . . .
We had something in common—the chopper. It was something
you either know or you don't know.
—TOM FUGLE, FOUNDING MEMBER OF EL FORASTERO
MOTORCYCLE CLUB

• • •

This bike is so comfortable it's like being in a La-Z-Boy with my
lady as a pillow behind me.
RICH HUNDLEY, SIXTY, OWNER OF A HARLEY-DAVIDSON
SOFTAIL CUSTOM

• • •

I know one couple who at sevety-six and seventy-five used
proceeds from their reverse mortgage and bought a new Harley-
Davidson motorcycle with a side car.
—PETER BELL

• • •

Before the surgery the doctor put me in position and cast a spinal curve that suited me for riding the bike. I guess you could call it a Harley curve.
—A Harley rider who continued riding after an accident requiring major surgery

• • •

Once, after a ten-day coma, I walked out of the hospital and straight to the Harley shop for a new bike. Man, you gotta get back on that steel stallion and ride.
—Frank Lockhart, who has ridden motorcycles since the age of ten

• • •

It's a special bike. It's not as comfortable as others, but it's much classier.
—José Valdez, who rides a Harley-Davidson Road King

• • •

PART THREE

WHERE TO?

The bike is a pen, the road, the rider's unfinished autobiography.
—Mark C. Taylor and José Marquez

• • •

Do not go where the path may lead, go instead where there is no path and leave a trail.
—Ralph Waldo Emerson

• • •

It's a world with 20,000 television channels. . . . Get as far away from it as you can.
—Honda ad

• • •

A journey is like marriage. The certain way to be wrong is to think you control it.
—John Steinbeck

• • •

Mmm, boy. This is the life! No more worries—no romantic hang-ups—no nothing! Just my whirling wheels—and the open road ahead of me!
—Captain America, from *Captain America* #130

• • •

When people asked me . . . why I had chosen to ride a motorcycle round the world, I had dozens of ingenious explanations. . . . The honest answer was too short and uncomfortable. I did it because I felt like it. All else followed from that.
—Ted Simon, from *Riding High*

• • •

The key to a good ride is to ride. You can't make memories sitting on a couch.
—STEVE REED, FROM *ROAD TALES*

• • •

Prepare. As a rule a first-time, multinational, transcontinental journey such as crossing Africa, the Americas, or Asia needs at the very least *one year* of preparation.
—CHRIS SCOTT, FROM *ADVENTURE MOTORCYCLING HANDBOOK*

• • •

The first commandment for every good explorer is that an expe-
dition has two points: the point of departure and the point of
arrival. If your intention is to make the second theoretical point
coincide with the actual point of arrival, don't think about the
means—because the journey is a virtual space that finishes when
it finishes, and there are as many means as there are different
ways of "finishing." That is to say, the means are endless.
—ERNESTO "CHE" GUEVARA, FROM *THE MOTORCYCLE
DIARIES*

• • •

Be careful going in search of adventure—it is
ridiculously easy to find.
—WILLIAM LEAST HEAT-MOON

• • •

We host several rides, the most notable being the 11-day, 11,000+ mile Iron Butt Rally. Additionally, the Iron Butt Association hosts the Saddle Sore 1000 (a 24-hour 1,000-mile ride), the Bun Burner 1500 (1,500 miles in 36 hours), the Bun Burner Gold (1,500 miles in 24 hours), the 50cc Quest (Cross Country in 50 hours or less), the National Parks Tour Master Traveler Award (visit 50 parks in at least 25 states), the coveted 10/10ths Challenge (10 consecutive 1,000 mile days) and the almost-impossible to get into 100K Club (100,000 miles or more in one year).
—STATEMENT OF PURPOSE FROM THE "IRON BUTT" ASSOCIATION

• • •

Trying for the Iron Butt on my bike was like running a 5K on one leg.
—SCOTT HATHAWAY, WHO RIDES A 1988 YAMAHA TÉNÉRÉ DUAL-SPORT

• • •

You have to have faith in this one goal, and when we all got together in Lisbon, it all gelled, suddenly all the pieces went together in the jigsaw. As we rolled through the whole thing, and everyone did their bit, and that's why we got through.
— Russ Malkin, on the Dakar Rally

• • •

By the end of the first day, we knew our simple idea to ride motorcycles across Asia had disappeared. Dehydrated, exhausted, lost, we were in some town we had never even seen on the map. The master route would be impossible, all that tying and retying of the red string was just wasted time. And we didn't care. The simple idea of not knowing where we were going next seemed more exciting.
—Peter Winter

• • •

The best way to gauge your touring-fatigue level, I've found, is to get off your bike for a minute and shut it off. If your head is humming like a tuning fork and you can't put change in a parking meter, it's probably time to stop. Dropped gloves are a bad sign, too.
—PETER EGAN

• • •

Nothing is better for your riding technique than twisty roads in the rain.
—NEIL PEART

• • •

Motorcycles make it easy to get out of the city and camp. And they're a hell of a lot cheaper than fancy cars.
—CASEY TORRANCE, WHO RODE THE CONTINENTAL DIVIDE FROM CANADA TO MEXICO ON A KAWASAKI KTM 450 MOTOCROSS BIKE

• • •

Try to become a custodian of your environment, somebody who uses it without destroying it—that, Virginia, is a relatively new point of view in our throw-away culture. You'll be able to take a measure of satisfaction in knowing that you're preserving a dwindling resource and keeping the sport enjoyable—and viable, too.
—BEN HANDS, *CYCLE MAGAZINE* (1970)

• • •

Where To?

Thanks to the Interstate Highway System, it is now possible to travel from coast to coast without seeing anything.
—Charles Kuralt

• • •

To mankind's age-old comment on the journey of life that the first one hundred years are the hardest, the traveler on a motorcycle can add that the first thousand miles are equally tough.
—Robert Edison Fulton Jr.

• • •

[I]t is time again to remind you that Baja is quite intolerant of those who ride beyond their abilities.
—CLEMENT SALVADORI

• • •

To me, the perfect motorcycling experience is getting up every morning knowing I'll be riding all day on roads and through scenery I've never seen before, to a destination I've never been, and with the knowledge that I'll be doing the same thing again tomorrow, and the next, and so on. If heaven exists, it will be like this for me.
—FRED RAU, FROM *MOTORCYCLE TOURING BIBLE*

• • •

Where To?

The stars streaked the night sky with light in that little mountain town and the silence and the cold dematerialised the darkness. It was as if all solid substances were spirited away in the ethereal space around us, denying our individuality and submerging us, rigid, in the immense blackness.
—ERNESTO "CHE" GUEVARA, FROM *THE MOTORCYCLE DIARIES*

• • •

Oh, public road, you express me better than I can express myself.
—WALT WHITMAN

• • •

Then spring came, the great time of traveling, and everybody in the scattered gang was getting ready to make one trip or another.
—JACK KEROUAC

• • •

PART FOUR

WHO RIDES?

Motorcycles represent different things to different people. For some folks, they represent basic transportation. To others, they represent the exhilaration of power and speed. To the humorless, they are a social irritation.
—DARWIN HOLMSTROM

• • •

The motorcyclist of a couple of decades ago [circa 1910] was a rather peculiar sort of fellow, who seldom thought twice before attempting to ride his little two-wheel steed over next-to-impossible obstacles, and [this] writer was no exception. In fact, in those days my greatest ambition was to see just how far my sleek machine would carry me into country never before penetrated by anything—a pack mule, a dog team, or an experienced man on foot. And, needless to say, it got me into plenty of trouble on numerous occasions.
—IVAN J. STRETTEN, FROM *MOTORCYCLE THRILLS*

• • •

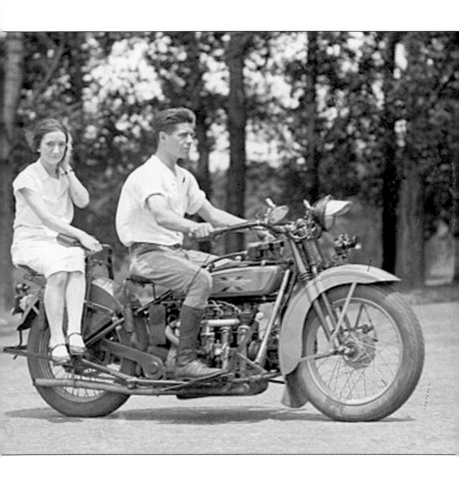

The sun has coated the trees and the grass and our cycles with a translucent yellow sheen, and we are all mesmerized by how we feel together; like a gigantic, roving thunderclap, leaning into the road, making the whole world tilt, eating up the macadam and concrete that snakes out in front of us.
—Lee Gutkind

• • •

I found myself flashing on the idea of doing this forever, riding motorbikes in our old age together.
—Ewan McGregor, on motorcycle riding with his wife

• • •

I've never ridden on a motorcycle before. It's fast. It scared me, but I forgot everything, it felt good. Is that what you do?
—Mary Murphy as Kathy to Marlon Brando's character, Johnny, in *The Wild One*

• • •

Black leather jackets were popular with American motorcyclists by the early 1950s, and hit the big time with the release of *The Wild One* in 1953. Marlon Brando's character, Johnny, epitomized this classic style.
—ROLAND BROWN

• • •

Milwaukee experienced more than a little hand-wringing in [the late 1960s], confronted by the fact that, in terms of public perception, the bad guys all rode Harleys.
—TOD RAFFERTY, FROM *HARLEY-DAVIDSON: THE ULTIMATE MACHINE*

• • •

Why do motorcycle gangs wear leather?

Because chiffon wrinkles so easily.
—OLD JOKE

• • •

The 1950s and 1960s saw the explosion of the American "motor-cycle culture," with black leather jackets becoming not only a statement of fashion, but of a preferred lifestyle.
—HARLEY-DAVIDSON PRESS RELEASE (1992)

● ● ●

Bury me in my leather jacket, jeans, and motorcycle boots.
—SID VICIOUS

● ● ●

Remember to rebel against authority, kids!
—HOMER SIMPSON, AS HE RIDES OFF ON A MOTORCYCLE IN
EPISODE 11, SEASON 8 OF *THE SIMPSONS*

● ● ●

Ever since World War II, California has been strangely plagued
by wild men on motorcycles.
—HUNTER S. THOMPSON

• • •

Gotta stop reading those hot-rod magazines, buddy. "Sickles" are
out—it's either a "bike" or a "motorcycle."
—ELVIS PRESLEY IN *ROUSTABOUT*

• • •

During those early years in New York, I often got on my motorcycle in the middle of the night and went for a ride—anyplace.
There wasn't much crime in the city then, and if you owned
a motorcycle, you left it outside your apartment and in the
morning it was still there. It was wonderful on summer nights
to cruise around the city at one, two, or three a.m. wearing jeans
and a t-shirt with a girl on the seat behind me. If I didn't start out
with one, I'd find one.
—MARLON BRANDO

• • •

The first thing you have to remember about motorcycles is that Marlon Brando can't possibly be riding every one you see.
—Ray Konkler, motorcycle dealer (1956)

• • •

Billy (Dennis Hopper): Man, everybody got chicken . . . Hey, we can't even get into a second-rate hotel, you dig? They think we're gonna cut their throats or something.

George (Jack Nicholson): They're not scared of you. They're scared of what you represent to 'em.

Billy: Hey, man, all we represent to them, man, is somebody who needs a haircut.

George: Oh no. What you represent to them is freedom.

—From *Easy Rider*

• • •

Valentino Rossi . . . thinks only of winning. It is why he is so good. Even at speed his mind is sedate enough to see the yellow flag. Focus. Think. Ride.
—Rick Broadbent, from *Ring of Fire*

• • •

I love beating my opponents on the last lap. It's the most exciting way to win a race. . . . You've studied your main opponent's trajectories, the way he takes every turn; you know where he's strongest and where his weaknesses are. You know where he's vulnerable if you attack him. . . . It's the ultimate rush.
—Valentino Rossi

• • •

I was a tomboy, the best at riding skateboards and bikes. Now I like riding motorcycles, riding them fast, doing wheelies and slides.
—Motorcycle stunt rider Debbie Evans

• • •

Who Rides?

My Dad rode motorcycles and he taught me how to ride when I
was six years old. I was so little I don't even remember learning
how to ride. I've just always been able to do it.
—MOTORCYCLE STUNT RIDER DEBBIE EVANS

• • •

I was just a kid walking to school when I saw this guy get hit
and this motorcycle guy was there just lying in the middle of the
street. I went up to him and he had blood coming from behind
his head. My first thought was: I've got to get a motorcycle.
There's something messed-up with my brain. . . .
—RYAN GOSLING

• • •

You're a Storm Rider 24/7. You may get a call at 2 a.m. from a
brother in need, and you better be ready to roll.
—A MEMBER OF THE STORM RIDER [ILLINOIS] MOTORCYCLE
CLUB

• • •

Trials riders are the musicians of the motorcycle world, tremendously skilled at what they do.
—Bruce Brown

• • •

The biggest hazard to a desert racer is another desert racer.
—Bruce Brown

• • •

[The rider is] the upper half of the motorcycle.
—Bernt Spiegel

• • •

I said that I wanted to get a motorcycle and one of the guys said, "You can't, girls don't ride motorcycles." I thought, "He shouldn't be telling a temperamental redhead what she can and cannot do." I had my permit within a week.
—MAGGIE MCNALLY, BOARD MEMBER OF THE AMERICAN MOTORCYCLIST ASSOCIATION

● ● ●

I hate riding on the back of a bike. It's a lot more fun being in control.
—CAM ARNOLD, VICE PRESIDENT OF THE MOTORCYCLE INDUSTRY COUNCIL

● ● ●

I kind of feel like I need to take on a role of getting it out there in public knowledge that women can ride. People assume that we're on the back of the bike making sandwiches.

—Tricia Helfer

• • •

They've heard it before from mothers, friends, brothers, and opinionated others: "Proper ladies don't ride on the backs of motorcycles." But no one ever said anything about riding on the front.

—Courtney Caldwell, an accountant, mother, and proud owner of a 550-pound, 700cc street cruiser

• • •

I need your clothes, your boots, and your motorcycle.
—ARNOLD SCHWARZENEGGER AS THE TERMINATOR IN *THE TERMINATOR*

• • •

If a typical worker makes a mistake seated at his job, he will likely not be thrown into a fence or have a half-dozen coworkers pile on top of him. This is why dirt track [motorcycle] racers often transition to other occupations.
—KRIS PALMER

• • •

I act. I am with my wife and kids. And I ride motorbikes. That's it, that's all I do.
—EWAN MCGREGOR

• • •

In LA, I have two cars and two motorcycles. In Italy, I have three motorcycles because other people want to ride and you can't ride them all at the same time.
—GEORGE CLOONEY

• • •

Owning a motorcycle used to be a lifestyle. Now, it's more a lifestyle accessory, like a cell phone or a fanny pack.
—JAY LENO

• • •

This is my anonymity. . . . With it, I'm just another a–hole on the streets.
—BRAD PITT, ON WEARING A MOTORCYCLE HELMET

• • •

Today, people have a lot more money to spend, and they're not learning how to ride. . . . It's like you just buy this rocket ship that you sit on.
—Jay Leno

• • •

In that moment of seamless happiness . . . the liberating joy of being astride a machine that would carry you like Odin's eight-legged horse in a whirl of noise and disapproving stares from straight folk was beyond my wildest dream.
—Joolz Denby, from *Billie Morgan*

• • •

And then there's the competitor. He lives and breathes motor-cycles. Eating, sex, things like that—all are secondary. He exists only for Sunday, when he can brutally punish his body for the privilege of winning a $283 trophy.
—Bob Sanford, from *Riding the Dirt*

• • •

I wanted to have a motorcycle, but I didn't want to miss the process of getting to that point. There was a lot to learn about myself and others before I would ever . . . ride in the open wind on a motorcycle. The journey matters.
—JOSEPH FEHLEN

• • •

Having spent ten years as an amateur . . . motorcycle racer, I know this from experience: racers see only what they need to see.
—MARK GARDINER, FROM *RIDING MAN*

• • •

There are times I prefer the solitude of a quiet day ride.
Sometimes one needs some alone time to sort out the
frustrations and puzzles of day-to-day life. Riding by yourself is
an excellent way to accomplish this.
—STEVE REED

• • •

The [Honda] 350 was tight and smooth and revvy and fast. The
little engine did all the right things. It was summer, in the Lakes
region of New Hampshire and even though we were riding two
up, which is not so cool, we didn't know or care any better.
—GORDON BUNKER

• • •

I don't ride a race, even today, where I don't feel like throwing up.
—MALCOLM SMITH

• • •

I never enter a race where I'm not counting my winnings a week before the event.
—MALCOLM SMITH

• • •

On the day of the race [the Baja 1000], the press was told that the first rider would arrive at the halfway point at around 5 a.m. Malcolm [Smith] arrived at 5 p.m., a full twelve hours earlier, and eight hours ahead of the next vehicle.
—DANA BROWN, FROM *DUST TO GLORY*

• • •

If a white guy wants to ride with a black club, most have no problem with it. The bikes and love of riding usually override everything else. Color is a weird thing. It just sort of goes away when you ride on two wheels.
—THE DIRECTOR OF MARKETING OUTREACH FOR HARLEY-DAVIDSON'S AFRICAN AMERICAN SEGMENT.

• • •

I know great people who have big bikes.
—A VATICAN SPOKESMAN AFTER POPE FRANCIS BLESSED 35,000 HARLEY-DAVIDSON RIDERS IN 2013

• • •

PART FIVE

STAYING SAFE

Thousands of people die from falling in their tubs every year, but no one tells you not to take a bath.
—SONNY BARGER

• • •

When I'm riding my motorcycle, I'm glad to be alive—and when I stop riding my motorcycle, I'm glad to be alive.
—NEIL PEART

• • •

There are only two kinds of bikers: those who have been down and those who are going down.
—ANONYMOUS

• • •

Cars are metal containers invented to trick you into feeling safe
in a big, scary world.
—A RIDER IN LAS VEGAS

• • •

Yes, but I've grown attached to my skin.
—A MOTORCYCLIST'S RESPONSE TO THE QUERY, "AREN'T YOU
HOT UNDER ALL THAT GEAR?"

• • •

Motorcycles trade safety for sensation, enclosure for exhilaration.
—KAREN LARSEN

• • •

Riding a motorcycle is like walking behind a horse. Don't do it unless you know that horse.
—Don Borkenhagen, sixty-five, who traded his motorcycle for a Honda Gold Wing Trike

• • •

My mother, like most moms, was deathly afraid of me getting on any motorcycle.
—Alton Brown

• • •

There's something eerie about a motorcycle lying on its side. It's unnatural.
—The owner of a 1970 Seeley, when the bike tipped over

• • •

All too often . . . cars collide with motorcycles. One of the most
frequently cited reasons is "failure to see," and these events are
so common that motorcyclists in England have taken to calling
them SMIDSYs, for "Sorry, Mate, I Didn't See You."
—TOM VANDERBILT, FROM *TRAFFIC: WHY WE DRIVE THE
WAY WE DO (AND WHAT IT SAYS ABOUT US)*

• • •

Having fallen and survived, the rider faces an important decision:
"Do I continue to ride?"
—MARK C. TAYLOR AND JOSÉ MARQUEZ

• • •

Once you go sideways, you never come back.
—POPULAR MOTORCYCLE LICENSE PLATE HOLDER

• • •

There are drunk riders. There are old riders. There are NO old, drunk riders.
—BUMPER STICKER

• • •

I was going faster than I ever went in my whole life, then I fell off.
—MICHAEL J. POLLARD AS LITTLE FAUSS IN *LITTLE FAUSS AND BIG HALSY*

• • •

[The Harley] dragbike with nitrous oxide injection . . . goes into a full tank slapper and just a few yards before the timing lights, spits me off. So I went through the lights at 139 mph, with an elapsed time of 10.52 seconds. But I was not on the bike.
—JOHN ULRICH, EDITOR, *ROADRACING WORLD*

• • •

[The] "loud pipes saves lives" approach [argues] that an ear-shattering exhaust system will surely alert drivers of [motorcycles'] presence. . . . [A] problem is that for the people who have to listen to the loud pipes, the issue of saving motorcyclists' lives might not exactly be a pressing agenda.
—TOM VANDERBILT, FROM *TRAFFIC: WHY WE DRIVE THE WAY WE DO (AND WHAT IT SAYS ABOUT US)*

• • •

Be as safe as you can while still having fun.
—NEAL PEART

• • •

I just never really applied for it. It was just one of those things that I never really did.
—GOVERNOR ARNOLD SCHWARZENEGGER, AFTER HE WAS INVOLVED IN A 2006 MOTORCYCLE ACCIDENT AND POLICE DISCOVERED THAT HE DID NOT HAVE A MOTORCYCLE LICENSE

• • •

I think art should be dangerous and uncomfortable and surprising and all those things *motorcycle* riding is.
—JEREMY IRONS

• • •

Come on, guys, we're exhausted. I think we should take the bikes back to the hotel, put them in a shed with the doors closed, and then play Scrabble in the room with the shades down.
—JOHN TRAVOLTA AS WOODY STEVENS IN *WILD HOGS*

• • •

If he was struck by lightning when he was riding his motorcycle, it was his *time*.
—THE WIDOW OF A MOTORCYCLIST STRUCK BY LIGHTNING WHILE RIDING HIS MOTORCYCLE

• • •

There is no such thing as bad [riding] weather, only the wrong clothes.
—Anonymous

• • •

But with the throttle screwed on there is only the barest margin and no room for mistakes. It has to be done right . . . and that's when the strange music starts, when you stretch your luck so far that the fear becomes exhilaration and vibrates along your arms. You can barely see at a hundred; the tears blow back so fast that they vaporize before they get to your ears. The only sounds are the wind and the dull roar floating back from the mufflers.
—Hunter S. Thompson

• • •

The burble of my exhaust unwound like a long cord behind me. Soon my speed snapped it, and I heard only the cry of the wind battering my head split and fended aside. The cry rose with my speed to a shriek while the air's coldness streamed like two jets of iced water into my dissolving eyes. . . . The next mile of road was rough. I braced my feet into the rests, thrust with my arms, and clenched my knees on the tank till its rubber grips goggled under my thighs. . . . The bad ground was passed and on the new road our flight became birdlike.
—T. E. Lawrence

• • •

If you ride fast and crash, you are a bad rider. If you go slow and crash, you are a bad rider. If you are a bad rider, you should not ride motorcycles.
—Hunter S. Thompson

• • •

Everyone crashes. Some get back on. Some don't. Some can't.
—ANONYMOUS

• • •

Never ride faster than your guardian angel can fly.
—ANONYMOUS

• • •

Insisting on perfect safety is for people who don't have the balls
to live in the real world.
—MARY SHAFER, NASA

• • •

Thin leather looks good in the bar, but it won't save your butt
from road rash if you go down.
—T-SHIRT

• • •

If you really want to know what's going on, watch what's happening at least five cars ahead.
—BUMPER STICKER

• • •

It's not the jump that's the scary part, it's the landing.
NEIL PEART, *GHOST RIDER*

• • •

I wanted to fly through the air. . . . One Mississippi, two Mississippi, three Mississippi, four Mississippi. You're in the air for four seconds, you're part of the machine, and then if you make a mistake midair, you say to yourself, "Oh, boy. I'm gonna crash," and there's nothing you can do to stop it.
—EVEL KNIEVEL

• • •

I want to die in my sleep, like my grandfather.
Not like my grandmother, who was in the sidecar.
—ANONYMOUS

• • •

I'd rather be riding my motorcycle thinking about God than sitting in church thinking about my motorcycle.
—ANONYMOUS

• • •

Does this bike make my butt look fast?
—POPULAR MOTORCYCLE T-SHIRT

• • •

Black care seldom sits behind a rider whose pace is fast enough.
—THEODORE ROOSEVELT

• • •

When a driver makes a sudden left turn in front of a motorcyclist and doesn't make it in time, we shouldn't expect to hear, *I saw you but I was in a hurry and I figured you'd get out of my way.*
—DAVID L. HOUGH, FROM *PROFICIENT MOTORCYCLING*

• • •

The most important reason for just swallowing your pride and getting out of the way is that cars and trucks are much bigger than bikes.
—DAVID L. HOUGH

• • •

Your only "reverse gear" [on a motorcycle] is pushing, so you don't want to be pointed downhill against a fence with boulders on both sides.
—NEIL PEART

• • •

Like most motorcyclists, my initial rider training (if I dare call it that) came in the form of a salesman pushing a bike off the showroom floor into the parking lot and pointing out the control features to me. . . . I went back to the dealership, wrote a check, and within a few minutes was out on my own, dicing my way through city traffic at rush hour. I'm very lucky to be alive today.
—DAVID L. HOUGH

• • •

At some time during your career as a dirt rider, you will involuntarily part company with your bike. Many times, probably.
—BOB SANFORD

• • •

Helmets take the spirit of freedom away.
—A HARLEY RIDER

• • •

The AMA believes that adults should have the right to voluntarily decide when to wear a helmet. . . . Many motorcyclists view the helmet as an accessory of personal apparel, and its use or non-use is connected with a chosen lifestyle and their right as adults to make their own decisions.
—STATEMENT BY THE AMERICAN MOTORCYCLIST ASSOCIATION REGARDING HELMET USE

• • •

I am personally sick and tired of hearing arguments about the constitutionality of helmet laws. . . . I would not ride without a helmet nor would I recommend anyone else doing so. Not even from your campsite to the Port-a-Potty.
—BOB SANFORD

• • •

Got a $5 head? Get a $5 helmet.
—BUMPER STICKER

• • •

Enough people weren't wearing [helmets], so we had to come up
with the helmet law. . . . The idea behind [it] is to preserve a brain
who's judgment is so poor, that it doesn't even try to prevent the
cracking of the head it's in!
—JERRY SEINFELD

• • •

Getting your bike stuck in the mud is bad enough. Getting your
body stuck in the mud is the worst—especially when it's your
girlfriend who has to dig you out.
—BRUCE BROWN

• • •

I have been riding BMW bikes for twenty years, but there are some basic techniques I have only learned now.
—JEREMY IRONS, AFTER COMPLETING A RIDER TRAINING COURSE IN 2013

• • •

I had been in a motorcycle accident and I'd been hurt, but I recovered. Truth was that I wanted to get out of the rat race.
—BOB DYLAN

• • •

I have a motorcycle prayer that I say before every ride.
—LAURENCE FISHBURNE

• • •

Loud pipes save lives!
—POPULAR LICENSE PLATE HOLDER

• • •

The [American Motorcyclist] Association believes that few other factors contribute more to misunderstanding and prejudice against the motorcycling community than excessively noisy motorcycles. A minority, riding loud motorcycles, may leave the impression that all motorcycles are loud. In fact, a significant percentage of the public does not realize that motorcycles are built to federally mandated noise control standards.
—AMERICAN MOTORCYCLIST ASSOCIATION POSITION ON
EXCESSIVE MOTORCYCLE NOISE

• • •

Motorcycle riders are safer [than drivers of cars]; they don't text
on their phones while riding.
—Paul Crowe

• • •

If you ride like there's no tomorrow, there won't be.
—Anonymous

• • •

WORKS AND AUTHORS QUOTED

Books

Steven E. Alford and Suzanne Ferriss
Motorcycle (2007)

Diana Bletter
The Mom Who Took Off on Her Motorcycle (2013)

Bolfert, Thomas C.
The Big Book of Harley-Davidson: Official Publication (1991)

Rick Broadbent
Ring of Fire: The Inside Story of Valentino Rossi and MotoGP
(2010)

Roland Brown
The Encyclopedia of Motorcycles: The Complete Book of Motorcycles and Their Riders (1996)

Gordon Bunker
The Making of a Motorcyclist (2011)

Beverly Cleary
The Mouse and the Motorcycle (2006)

Keith Code
A Twist of the Wrist (1983)

Willie G. Davidson
100 Years of Harley-Davidson (2002)

Joolz Denby
Billie Morgan (2005)

Peter Egan
Leanings: The Best of Peter Egan from Cycle World Magazine (2009)
Leanings 2: Great Stories by America's Favorite Motorcycle Writer (2005)

Joseph Fehlen
Ride On: A Motorcycle Journey to Awaken the Soul and Rediscover Its Meaning (2012)

Works and Authors Quoted

Robert Edison Fulton Jr.
One Man Caravan (1937, 1996)

Mark Gardiner
Riding Man (2012)

Ernesto "Che" Guevara
The Motorcycle Diaries: Notes on a Latin American Journey (2003)

Guggenheim Museum
The Art of the Motorcycle (1999)

Lee Gutkind
Bike Fever (1973)

John Hall
Riding on the Edge (2011)

Ajit Harisinghani
One Life to Ride (2010)

Thomas Hauffe
Design: A Concise History (1998)

James Hesketh
Riding on a Straight and Twisty Road (2011)

Melissa Holbrook Pierson
The Perfect Vehicle: What is it About Motorcycles? (1998)

*The Man Who Would Stop at Nothing: Long Distance
Motorcycling's Endless Road* (2011)

Darwin Holmstrom
Complete Idiot's Guide to Motorcycles (1998)

David L. Hough
Proficient Motorcycling (2000)

Jeremy Kroeker
Motorcycle Therapy: A Canadian Adventure in Central America
(2006)

Richard La Plante
Hog Fever (1997)

Karen Larsen
*Breaking the Limit: One Woman's Motorcycle Journey Through
North America* (2004)

Daniel Meyer
Life Is a Road: The Soul is a Motorcycle (2003)

Nathan Milwand
The Long Ride "Home" (2012)

Ewan McGregor and Charley Boorman
Long Way Round: Casting Shadows Across the World (2005)
*Long Way Down: An Epic Journey by Motorcycle from Scotland to
South Africa* (2009)

Works and Authors Quoted

Kris Palmer
Motorcycle Survivor: Tips and Tales in the Unrestored Realm
(2010)

Neil Peart
Far and Away: A Prize Every Time (2011)
Ghost Rider: Travels on the Healing Road (2002)

Brian Pechtl
Of Motorcycles and Brothers (2012)

Dave Preston
Motorcycle 201 (2010)

Lois Pryce
Lois on the Loose (2012)

Tod Rafferty
Harley-Davidson: The Ultimate Machine (2002)

Joel Rappaport
Hopeless Class (2012)

Fred Rau
The Motorcycle Touring Bible (2011)

Steve Reed
Road Tales (2008)

Mark Richardson
Zen and Now: On the Trail of Robert Pirsig and the Art of Motorcycle Maintenance (2008)

Valentino Rossi and Enrico Borghi
What If I Had Never Tried It? (2009)

Clement Salvadori
Motorcycle Journeys Through Baja (1997)

Bob Sanford
Riding the Dirt (1972)

Chris Scott
Adventure Motorcycling Handbook (2012)

Ted Simon
Jupiter's Travels: Four Years Around the World on a Triumph (1979)
Riding High (1998)

Ivan G. Stretten
Motorcycle Thrills (1950)

Patrick Symmes
Chasing Che: A Motorcycle Journey in Search of the Guevara Legend (2000)

Hunter S. Thompson
Hell's Angels: A Strange and Terrible Saga (1966)

Works and Authors Quoted

Kingdom of Fear: Loathsome Secrets of a Star-Crossed Child in the Final Days of the American Century (2003)
"Song of the Sausage Creature," *Cycle World* (1995)

Tom Vanderbilt
Traffic: Why We Drive the Way We Do (and What it Says About Us) (2008)

Dziga Vertov
The Writings of Dziga Vertov (1984)

Will Wilkins and Kate Macdonell
Wollongong to Woolwich (2012)

Hugo Wilson
The Encyclopedia of the Motorcycle (1995)

Films

Biker Boyz (2003)
Dust to Glory (2007)
Easy Rider (1969)
Electra Glide in Blue (1973)
Little Fauss and Big Halsy (1970)
Motorcycle Karma (2009)
On Any Sunday (1971)
The Terminator (1984)
Wild Hogs (2007)
The Wild One (1954)

Periodicals

American Motorcyclist
The Business Journal Serving Greater Milwaukee
Cycle World
Harpers
Hog Magazine
Huffington Post
International Journal of Motorcycle Studies
Los Angeles Herald Examiner
Los Angeles Times
Maxim
Motorcyclist Magazine
New York Daily News
The *New York Times*
Roadracing World
Rider
Salon
Slate
Throttler Magazine
U.S. Rider News
Vintage Guitar Magazine
Vogue (Italy)

Web sites

http://www.americanmotorcyclist.com/
http://www.bmwmotorcycles.com
http://www.entertainmentwise.com
http://www.europeanmotorcycle-diaries.com/
http://www.harley-davidson.com

Works and Authors Quoted

http://www.ironbutt.com

http://thekneeslider.com/10-reasons-motorcycles-are-better-than-cars/

http://www.menshealth.com/

http://www.motorcyclemuseum.org/

http://www.orangecountychoppers.com/

http://realwomenandmotorcycles.com/

http://www.studio360.org/2010/oct/15/harley-davidson/transcript/

INDEX

PHOTO CREDITS

Page xii Thinkstock/John Foxx

Page 4: Library of Congress/ National Photo Company Collection

Page 7: Thinkstock/Hemera

Pages 8–9: Thinkstock/iStockphoto

Page 10: iStockphoto

Page 13: Courtesy of the author

Page 14: Thinkstock/iStockphoto

Page 16–17: Thinkstock/Digital Vision

Page 20: Library of Congress/ Herman A. French Collection

Page 25: Thinkstock/iStockphoto

Pages 28–29: Thinkstock/ iStockphoto

Page 31: Courtesy of the author

Pages 34–35: Thinkstock/ iStockphoto

Page 38: Courtesy of the author

Page 46: Thinkstock/iStockphoto

Page 49: Library of Congress/ Herman A. French Collection

Pages 50–51: Thinkstock/ iStockphoto

Page 54: Library of Congress/U.S. Office of War Information

Pages 58–59: Library of Congress/ Harris & Ewing Collection

Page 63: Courtesy of the author

Page 66: Courtesy of the author

Pages 67–68: Thinkstock/Comstock

Page 71: Courtesy of the author

Page 72: Thinkstock/iStockphoto

Page 75: Courtesy of the author

Page 78: Courtesy of the author

Page 81: Thinkstock/iStockphoto

Pages 82–83: Thinkstock

Page 85: Courtesy of the author

Pages 90–91: Thinkstock/Digital Vision

Pages 96–97: Thinkstock/Monkey Business

Pages 100–101: Thinkstock/Digital Vision

Page 104: Thinkstock/iStockphoto

Page 107: Library of Congress/Herman A. French Collection

Page 108: Thinkstock/IStockphoto

Pages 110–111: Thinkstock/Digital Vision

Page 113: Thinkstock/iStockphoto

Page 114: Thinkstock/Polka Dot

Pages 118–119: Thinkstock/iStockphoto

Page 121: Courtesy of the author

Pages 124–125: Thinkstock/iStockphoto

Pages 128–129: Thinkstock/iStockphoto

Page 130: Thinkstock/IStockphoto

Page 133: Library of Congress/Herman A. French Collection

Pages 136–137: Thinkstock/iStockphoto

Page 138: Thinkstock/Ablestock.com

Pages 142–143: Thinkstock/Digital Vision

Page 145: Thinkstock/iStockphoto

Page 146: Library of Congress/George Grantham Bain Collection

Page 148: Courtesy of the author

Page 153: Library of Congress/LC-USZC4-3030

Pages 160–161: Thinkstock/iStockphoto

Page 162: Thinkstock/Ablestock.com

Page 165: Thinkstock/iStockphoto

Page 168: Courtesy of the author

Pages 172–173: Thinkstock/iStockphoto

Page 177: Thinkstock/Ablestock.com

Page 182: Courtesy of the author

Page 185: Courtesy of the author

Pages 188–189: Thinkstock/iStockphoto

Page 191: Courtesy of the author

Pages 194–195: Thinkstock/iStockphoto

Page 196: Thinkstock/iStockphoto

Page 206: Courtesy of the author